WINDOWS OF INFLUENCE

THE BATTLE FOR THE HEART OF MAN

Betzy Cordoba

Manos Unidas Foundation
SAN FRANCISCO, CALIFORNIA

Ordering Information:
Special discounts for bulk purchases are available for corporations, associa-tions, churches, and other groups. For more information, contact the Spe-cial Sales Department at the address listed above.
ISBN: 9798304375719

Windows of Influence: The Battle for the Heart of Man / Betzy Cordoba. –
1st ed.

To my Lord and Savior, Jesus Christ, who took my broken heart and transformed it with His love and grace. To Him, who rescued me from the poor, the vile, and the despised of the world, and brought me into the newness of life in His truth. To Him, I give all honor and glory for the unmerited privilege of taking up a pen to write about His eternal truth.

To my pastor and covering, who has been a father, teacher, and guide during these formative years, patiently and wisely modeling the character of Christ in my life. To my beloved husband, for his sacrifice, unconditional support, and patience throughout this journey. To my daughters and grandchildren, who lovingly continue to offer their time and presence so that I can fulfill the calling God has placed on my life.

To the church where I was shaped, my family in the faith, thank you for being a place of growth, love, and fellowship. Each of you has been an instrument of God to strengthen me along this path. This work is an expression of gratitude to all who have walked with me in this mission.

To God be all the glory.

"And do not be conformed to this world, but be transformed by the renewing of your mind, that you may prove what is the good and acceptable and perfect will of God."
—Romans 12:2

Index

The Power of Cinema and Television as Ideology Shapers: A Christian Perspective

"You are the light of the world. A city on a hill cannot be hidden."

Matthew 5:14

INTRODUCTION

The Power of Cinema and Television as Ideology Shapers: A Christian Perspective

Since their inception, cinema and television have not only been windows to the world but also mirrors and hammers that shape societies. Over the last few decades, these tools have transcended their original purpose of entertainment to become powerful vehicles for ideological transmission. Beyond informing, visual media shape what audiences perceive as acceptable, desirable, or even inevitable. This phenomenon, described by Noam Chomsky as the "Manufacture of Consent," is complemented by the "Overton Window" theory, which explains how ideas once deemed unthinkable gradually become accepted and eventually dominant.

The influence of these visual narratives is far from neutral. Through carefully crafted stories and characters, cinema and television have played a crucial role in redefining fundamental values such as family, gender, morality, and faith. This cultural transformation is not accidental; it responds to an intentional project seeking to uproot eternal truths and replace them with relative and subjective values. Here lies the subversive power of these tools: they not only present a narrative but also shape collective consciousness, challenging God's design.

As Christians, we cannot ignore this reality. Ephesians 5:21-25 reminds us that the family, according to God's design, is a space of sacrificial love and mutual service. This model starkly contrasts with the individualistic and fragmenting narratives that dominate modern audiovisual culture. This book aims to expose how cinema and television have contributed to the erosion of biblical values and to offer a response rooted in the restoration of God's design.

A Chronological Journey: From Challenge to Restoration

Throughout this book, we explore how cinema and television have influenced social perceptions from the 1950s to the present day. We analyze how these tools have been used to fragment the family, redefine masculinity and femininity, and distort biblical principles of unity, love, and service. Each chapter unpacks how these narratives were designed to displace God from the center of society, replacing Him with a fluid morality that appeals to cultural relativism.

In the light of Scripture, we challenge these narratives and present a hopeful vision: the restoration of society through a return to the eternal principles of God's Kingdom. Proverbs 22:6 reminds us of the importance of training future generations in the right way so that even in times of confusion, they will not stray from it. This book invites Christians not to be passive spectators but to take an active role in the cultural battle, using the same communication tools to proclaim the truth and restore God's values.

The Call to Action

This book is not just an analysis but also a call to action. Romans 12:2 exhorts us: "Do not conform to the pattern of this world but be transformed by the renewing of your mind." This command guides every chapter: to discern the ideologies shaping culture and respond with creativity, faithfulness, and courage.

The task of restoring truth in a world saturated with lies is not easy, but it is possible. Through practical examples and strategies inspired by biblical principles, this book seeks to equip believers to use cinema, television, and digital media as platforms to counter destructive narratives and proclaim God's perfect design for humanity.

The Great Commission (Matthew 28:19-20) calls us not only to make disciples but to disciple nations. This mandate includes shaping cultures and systems to reflect God's justice, grace, and truth. May this book serve as a tool to inspire, challenge, and mobilize the Church to act as a living and dynamic body committed to restoring God's design in all spheres of society.

"For we are God's handiwork, created in Christ Jesus to do good works, which God prepared in advance for us to do"

(Ephesians 2:10). May this work inspire every reader to rise with purpose, embrace their role in this generation, and boldly proclaim God's eternal truth.

The Early Challenges to Marriage and the Traditional Family

"Therefore a man shall leave his father and his mother and hold fast to his wife, and they shall become one flesh."

Genesis 2:24

1950'S

CHAPTER 1

1950s The Early Challenges to Marriage and the Traditional Family

The Ideal of the Nuclear Family and the First Cultural Cracks

The 1950s represented an apparent heyday for the nuclear family model. This structure, composed of a breadwinning father, a homemaking mother, and children as the center of family life, was widely idealized. However, while the social surface presented a robust and orderly home, cultural forces in the background were beginning to challenge this conception.

The Bible establishes in Genesis 2:24: "Therefore a man shall leave his father and his mother and hold fast to his wife, and they shall become one flesh." This design by God emphasizes unity, commitment, and complementarity as essential foundations of the family. However, mass media, especially cinema and television, began to promote narratives that, while subtle, challenged these principles. This initial questioning was not accidental; rather, it formed part of an orchestrated cultural shift that would use entertainment as a tool to progressively dismantle traditional values.

Teenage Romanticism and the Rise of Individualism

Iconic films such as Rebel Without a Cause (1955) and A Summer Place (1959) marked the beginning of a change in cultural narratives. Rebel Without a Cause, starring James Dean, portrayed a teenager in conflict with paternal authority. Instead of presenting the father as a figure of wisdom and moral leadership, he was shown as distant and ineffective. This approach symbolized a generation that began to reject traditional norms and embrace a spirit of autonomy and rebellion.

Meanwhile, A Summer Place introduced teenage sexuality as a central theme. The film depicted premarital relationships without moral condemnation, desacralizing intimacy and severing it from its marital context. This narrative contributed to normalizing the idea that love, and sexual desire could exist outside the bounds of marriage, breaking with the biblical teaching of the sanctity of sexuality (1 Corinthians 6:18-20).

Both films reflect an ideological deconstruction strategy, where cinema served as a means to dissociate love from responsibility, exalting individualism and the pursuit of personal happiness over collective commitments. This cultural shift contrasted with teachings such as Ephesians 5:25: "Husbands, love your wives, just as Christ loved the church and gave himself up for her," which demand sacrificial and committed love.

The Transformation of Family Roles: Questioning and Tension

In the 1950s, cinema also began to reformulate family roles. Women, traditionally represented as mothers and wives, were progressively portrayed as dissatisfied with their domestic roles. Although these narratives were nascent, they planted the seeds for feminist debates in the following decades.

Simultaneously, the father figure was subjected to critical revision. Films and programs portrayed men who, far from being strong leaders and protectors, were depicted as vulnerable or ineffective. This narrative shift reflected an emerging crisis of masculinity, eroding the patriarchal model of the home as a space of leadership and protection. From a Christian perspective, this contradicted the teaching of 1 Corinthians 11:3, which establishes God's order for the family.

The Role of Media in the Manufacture of Cultural Change

The concept of "Manufacture of Consent," proposed by Noam Chomsky, is key to understanding the impact of 1950s cinema and television. During this decade, the media did not directly attack traditional family values but began to subtly displace them. Narratives prioritized personal desire over collective commitment, promoting cultural change that would fully unfold in the subsequent decades.

A significant example is the program I Love Lucy (1951–1957). Although it seemingly portrayed a traditional family, it also introduced elements of humor that trivialized marital tensions. By doing so, it normalized questioning traditional family dynamics. This approach laid the groundwork for more disruptive narratives that would openly challenge Judeo-Christian values in the future.

The Ideological Narrative Behind Cultural Productions

From a broad perspective, the narratives of the 1950s did not arise in a vacuum. They were rooted in an ideological agenda aimed at transforming society from within. Early feminism and Marxist theses on the deconstruction of traditional institutions found a powerful ally in cinema. These movements understood that cultural change required the erosion of the family, seen as a fundamental pillar of social order.

Antonio Gramsci, one of the most prominent Marxist theorists for his contributions to concepts such as cultural hegemony, hegemonic blocs, and postmodernism in relation to consumer society, proposed that, rather than imposing change by force, ideas should infiltrate collective consciousness through key institutions such as cinema and education. The 1950s marked the beginning of this strategy.

A Christian Perspective on Cultural Change

From a Christian perspective, the cultural shift of the 1950s represented a departure from God's design for the family. Deuteronomy 6:6-7 calls on parents to pass on God's truths to future generations, underscoring the family's role as a means of preserving spiritual values. However, cultural narratives began to divert this focus, suggesting that individuals should find their own path regardless of the teachings received at home.

Rather than reflecting the relationship between Christ and His church, as described in Ephesians 5:22-33, cultural narratives promoted a view of the family as a flexible and, in some cases, dispensable structure. This posed a direct challenge to the church and believers, who were called to resist this trend and model biblical principles in their own homes.

The cultural legacy of the 1950s was not limited to its immediate impact but laid the groundwork for the social transformations of subsequent decades. By introducing the questioning of gender roles, the exaltation of individualism, and the desacralization of sexuality, this decade marked the beginning of a process that would redefine perceptions of family and morality in Western culture.

1960'S

The Second Wave
of Feminism and
the Beginning of
the Cultural Revolution

"So God created man in his own image, in the image of God he created him; male and female he created them."
Genesis 1:27

CHAPTER 2

1960s: The Second Wave of Feminism and the Beginning of the Cultural Revolution

The Unleashing of a Cultural Revolution

The 1960s marked a radical shift in the cultural and social structures that had defined Western society. The Second Wave of Feminism, along with counterculture and the sexual revolution, became key movements for redefining values surrounding gender, family, and sexuality. In this context, cinema and television served not only as mirrors of this transformation but also as catalysts that promoted new ideologies and questioned the Judeo-Christian foundations of social order.

Emerging feminism sought not only equality but began to reconsider the very nature of gender roles. Simone de Beauvoir's phrase, "One is not born, but rather becomes, a woman," marked a turning point as it challenged God's design of man and woman as unique and complementary creations. In contrast, Genesis 1:27 reaffirms: "So God created man in his own image, in the image of God he created him; male and female he created them." This conflict between a biblical worldview and humanist ideas sparked a cultural battle that would redefine notions of family, sexuality, and gender.

Feminism and the Deconstruction of Traditional Roles

The Second Wave of Feminism expanded the demands of its predecessors, focusing on personal autonomy, reproductive control, and gender equality in all aspects of life. In this scenario, cinema played a crucial role in questioning traditional values and normalizing a vision of women as independent from family roles.

Films like Rosemary's Baby (1968) and The Apartment (1960) became emblematic of this cultural shift. Rosemary's Baby portrayed marriage as an oppressive and secretive structure where the protagonist is manipulated and used without her consent. The narrative implied that traditional institutions like family could be dangerous and limiting. In The Apartment, Shirley MacLaine's protagonist highlighted workplace gender inequalities while introducing the idea that women's personal fulfillment lies beyond the home.

Both films began to fragment the perception of the family as a safe space and proposed that individual satisfaction should be prioritized. From a biblical perspective, this shift clashed with principles like those in Ephesians 5:22-25, which calls husbands to love their wives sacrificially and wives to live in a relationship of love and mutual respect. However, the cultural narratives of the decade promoted autonomy over family interdependence.

The Cultural Impact of Cinema on Collective Morality

The cinema of the 1960s embraced the sexual revolution, using its narratives to normalize the idea of personal freedom as the highest good. In films like Bonnie and Clyde (1967), characters who rejected traditional social norms, including gender roles, were glorified. Bonnie, a woman living outside the law, was portrayed as a symbol of freedom, breaking away from traditional expectations of femininity.

This cultural shift contrasted with biblical teachings about sexuality, as seen in 1 Corinthians 6:18: "Flee from sexual immorality. Every other sin a person commits is outside the body, but the sexually immoral person sins against his own body." While the Bible affirms sexuality as a sacred gift within marriage, the films of the decade presented intimacy as an experience devoid of commitment or moral responsibility.

The Family Under Attack: Cinema as a Tool of Deconstruction

The representation of family in 1960s cinema began to crumble. Films no longer depicted family unity as the core of stability but as an obstacle to self-realization. Marriage was no longer seen as a sacred covenant but as a negotiable institution adaptable to individual circumstances.

Movies like Guess Who's Coming to Dinner (1967) addressed family tensions from generational and cultural perspectives, while other productions began normalizing divorce, open relationships, and infidelity as acceptable responses to personal crises. This direct attack on God's design for marriage contradicts passages such as Matthew 19:6: "So they are no longer two but one flesh. What therefore God has joined together, let not man separate." Cinema became a vehicle for normalizing family fragmentation, eroding its purpose as the place for spiritual and moral formation.

The Seeds of Moral Fragmentation

The 1960s not only transformed cultural narratives but also planted the seeds of deeper moral fragmentation that would impact subsequent generations. By exalting personal autonomy, cinema and television weakened family bonds and promoted a vision of life centered on the individual.

From a Christian perspective, this period underscores the need to reaffirm eternal principles about God's design for family and sexuality. In the face of a culture that glorifies hedonism and self-definition, Scripture calls us to a higher standard, as found in Romans 12:2: "Do not be conformed to this world, but be transformed by the renewal of your mind, that by testing you may discern what is the will of God, what is good and acceptable and perfect."

The 1960s not only marked the beginning of a cultural revolution but also an outright assault on Christian values regarding family, marriage, and sexuality. Cinema, as a powerful tool of influence, shaped mindsets and presented narratives that exalted autonomy and rejection of authority. These ideas, though seemingly liberating, began to blur God's perfect design for society.

Let us remember that cultural change is not neutral; it responds to ideological forces seeking to replace God's order with human constructs. However, as Christians, we are called to be salt and light in a generation that needs to rediscover the truth and beauty of God's design. Understanding history and cultural strategies equips us to respond with discernment and boldly proclaim that true freedom is found in Christ and His eternal truth.

1970's

Abortion and the Breakdown of Family Commitment

"For you created my inmost being; you knit me together in my mother's womb."
Psalm 139:13

CHAPTER 3

1970s: Abortion and the Breakdown of Family Commitment

The Consolidation of a Cultural Revolution: Roe v. Wade and Cinema as an Ideological Vehicle

The 1970s marked a turning point in Western culture, characterized by the rise of movements that directly challenged traditional Judeo-Christian values. The historic 1973 Roe v. Wade ruling, which legalized abortion in the United States, represented a radical shift in the perception of life and family commitment. This event, far from being merely a legal matter, reconfigured the moral foundations of society, becoming a catalyst for a new cultural narrative that exalted individual autonomy over the sanctity of life and unbreakable commitments.

Cinema, as a mass medium, played a crucial role in this shift, reflecting and promoting the ideologies that supported this transformation. Films like The Stepford Wives (1975) and Love with the Proper Stranger (1963) began to portray motherhood, marriage, and family life not as essential pillars of society but as negotiable choices subject to individual desires and circumstances. In The Stepford Wives, the family is depicted as an oppressive institution, symbolized by women deprived of personal agency. This message, though disguised as social critique, prepared audiences to accept a redefinition of gender roles and marital commitment.

From a Christian perspective, this cultural shift stands in direct opposition to biblical teachings on the sanctity of life and the intrinsic value of family. Psalm 139:13-16 proclaims: "For you created my inmost being; you knit me together in my mother's womb... Your eyes saw my unformed body." However, the cultural narratives of the 1970s downplayed the importance of these truths, normalizing a worldview centered on the individual and disconnected from God's design.

Abortion and the Redefinition of Motherhood

Roe v. Wade not only established a legal precedent but also fueled a cultural shift that redefined motherhood. Starting in the 1970s, films began to depict pregnancy as a potential burden rather than a gift from God. Productions like Love with the Proper Stranger portrayed women facing unwanted pregnancies, presenting motherhood as a limitation to personal fulfillment. Instead of valuing the inherent sacrifice of being a mother, these narratives promoted the idea that motherhood should be a choice based solely on individual desire.

This cultural shift contrasts with the teachings of Scripture, which elevate motherhood to a God-given calling filled with purpose. Psalm 127:3 reminds us: "Children are a heritage from the Lord, offspring a reward from him." Yet, the cultural narratives of the 1970s began to undermine this understanding, presenting children as an optional choice rather than a divine blessing.

The Crisis of Marital Commitment

The cinema of the 1970s also reflected a growing crisis in the perception of marriage. Films like Kramer vs. Kramer (1979) depicted divorce as a pragmatic solution to marital tensions, normalizing the idea that marital commitments could be discarded if they no longer met individual needs. This narrative marked a departure from the biblical concept of marriage as a sacred and indissoluble covenant. Matthew 19:6 states: "So they are no longer two, but one flesh. Therefore, what God has joined together, let no one separate."

The cinematic productions of this decade fostered a perception of marriage as a flexible institution, in contrast to biblical teachings that present it as a permanent commitment rooted in sacrificial love and faithfulness. This pragmatic approach weakened God's model for marriage, prioritizing emotions and individual desires over the values of permanence and sacrifice.

Relationships Without Commitment: The Exaltation of Individual Autonomy

Continuing the trend initiated in the 1960s, the cinema of the 1970s continued to exalt non-committal relationships as an ideal of personal freedom. Films like Bob & Carol & Ted & Alice (1969) set a precedent for the portrayal of open relationships, promoting the idea that intimacy could be separated from commitment. This type of narrative directly challenged the biblical vision of marriage and sexuality, as presented in Proverbs 5:18-19: "May your fountain be blessed, and may you rejoice in the wife of your youth. A loving doe, a graceful deer—may her breasts satisfy you always, may you ever be intoxicated with her love."

These portrayals reinforced the idea that personal satisfaction should prevail over any form of responsibility or exclusivity, blurring the fundamental values of marital love and faithfulness.

The Redefinition of Male Roles and the Fragmentation of Fatherhood

While women in films gained autonomy and freedom, men began to be portrayed as conflicted figures, struggling to find their place within a transforming family structure. Films like An Unmarried Woman (1978) explored the dynamics of women thriving after divorce, relegating male characters to secondary or irrelevant roles. This cultural shift eroded the perception of men as leaders and protectors within the family unit.

From a biblical perspective, male leadership is rooted in sacrificial love and service, as taught in Ephesians 5:25: "Husbands, love your wives, just as Christ loved the church and gave himself up for her." However, 1970s cinema challenged this model, presenting men as figures in decline and marriage as a disposable contract.

The Legacy of the 1970s on Family Culture

The 1970s consolidated many of the changes initiated in the 1960s, promoting a cultural narrative centered on personal autonomy and the freedom of choice. Through cinema, ideologies were disseminated that fragmented Judeo-Christian values concerning family, marriage, and sexuality, preparing society for even greater disintegration in subsequent decades.

While Scripture offers a vision of the family as a divine institution designed to reflect God's love and faithfulness, the cultural narratives of the 1970s promoted a perspective in which personal satisfaction and autonomy prevailed over any other commitment. This contrast underscores the need to return to God's design to find true stability and purpose amidst a constantly changing culture.

The Normalization of Abortion and Teenage Sexuality

1980'S

"Flee from sexual immorality. Every other sin a person commits is outside the body, but the sexually immoral person sins against his own body."
1 Corinthians 6:18

<u>CHAPTER 4</u>

1980s – The Normalization of Abortion and Teenage Sexuality

Individualism and the Fragmentation of Family Values

The 1980s represented a profound transformation in cultural and family values, consolidating individualism as the guiding principle of an evolving society. Personal success and self-sufficiency began to overshadow traditional values of sacrifice, commitment, and collective responsibility. This shift, driven by economic growth, globalization, and consumer culture, found ideal vehicles for propagating these new narratives in cinema and television.

Films such as Dirty Dancing (1987), Nine to Five (1980), and Wall Street (1987) not only captured the spirit of the era but also promoted an ideology that exalted personal fulfillment above family and spiritual values. The dissociation between sexuality, motherhood, and God's purpose became evident, shaping a generation toward the pursuit of individual autonomy as the ultimate goal.

Abortion as an Acceptable Narrative: Dirty Dancing (1987)

One of the decade's most controversial representations was the normalization of abortion within romantic storylines. In Dirty Dancing (1987), the subplot involving Penny, a young woman who undergoes a clandestine abortion, is treated with a narrative detachment that avoids reflecting on the value of life or the moral implications. Abortion is presented as a practical solution to a "problem," a way to allow the main plot to proceed without disruption.

This representation legitimized abortion culturally as a necessary choice for personal freedom, stripping the act of its ethical and spiritual implications. Isaiah 44:24 reminds us: "This is what the Lord says—your Redeemer, who formed you in the womb: I am the Lord, the Maker of all things..." However, this message was displaced by a narrative prioritizing individual autonomy over the sanctity of life.

Teenage Sexuality and the Dissociation of Responsibility

The cinema of the 1980s marked a significant shift in the portrayal of sexuality, particularly among teenagers. Films like Fast Times at Ridgemont High (1982) and Dirty Dancing depicted sexuality as an inevitable rite of passage, disconnected from commitment and from emotional or spiritual consequences. These narratives exalted sexual freedom as an expression of identity and self-discovery, promoting a perspective where intimacy lacked moral context.

In contrast, biblical teaching calls for purity and respect for the body as a temple of the Holy Spirit. 1 Corinthians 6:18 exhorts: "Flee from sexual immorality... glorify God with your body." However, the cultural representations of the 1980s dismissed these principles, suggesting that immediate gratification and personal freedom were the predominant values.

The Working Woman: Nine to Five (1980) and the Redefinition of Femininity

The rise of feminism during the 1980s found emblematic representation in films like Nine to Five (1980) and Working Girl (1988). These stories narrated the struggles of women striving for professional success in male-dominated environments, exalting economic independence and autonomy as pillars of modern femininity.

While these films reflected significant advances in terms of equal opportunities, they also promoted a vision of femininity that relegated motherhood and marriage to secondary roles. In contrast, biblical teaching values the balance between family and vocational roles. Titus 2:4-5 instructs women to "love their husbands and children," recognizing the importance of the home as a sphere of divine influence. However, the cultural narratives of the 1980s began to redefine femininity in a

way that placed individual success above family responsibilities.

Consumer Culture and the Pursuit of Personal Success: Wall Street (1987)

Materialism and individualism found their ultimate expression in films like Wall Street (1987). The character of Gordon
Gekko, with his famous line "Greed is good," became the symbol of a generation obsessed with financial success and the
accumulation of power. This narrative promoted the idea that
self-fulfillment could only be achieved through unbridled ambition and self-sufficiency.

However, this pursuit of material success often came at
the expense of family and community values. Scripture offers
a radically different perspective. Philippians 2:3-4 teaches:
"Do nothing out of selfish ambition... value others above yourselves." The biblical narrative emphasizes that true success
lies in service, sacrifice, and building meaningful relationships,
rather than in the accumulation of wealth.

The Fragmentation of Family Values and Spiritual Erosion

The 1980s consolidated a cultural shift that began to blur
the lines between the sacred and the secular, between commitment and convenience. Motherhood ceased to be seen as
a gift from God and was instead presented as a negotiable

option. Sexuality was stripped of its context of responsibility, and the family, as an institution, began to lose its central position in cultural narratives.

From a Christian perspective, this period serves as a warning about the dangers of straying from God's design. Biblical teaching calls us to value life, purity, and commitment as essential virtues for a healthy society. Psalm 127:3 declares: "Children are a heritage from the Lord, offspring a reward from him." Yet the narratives of the 1980s ignored this truth, promoting a vision centered on individual autonomy and moral relativism.

The Legacy of the 1980s on Family Culture

The impact of 1980s cinema and television extended beyond its historical moment, establishing a cultural precedent that continues to resonate today. By normalizing abortion, exalting sexual freedom, and redefining family roles, this decade prepared the ground for a society that prioritizes immediate gratification and individual independence over the values of community, sacrifice, and responsibility.

This legacy presents profound challenges for those seeking to live according to God's design in a world that has embraced relativism as the norm. The biblical narrative offers a radically different alternative: a life centered on service, faithfulness, and obedience to eternal principles. In a cultural context where individualism has become the supreme ideal, the church has the responsibility to be a beacon of truth and hope, reminding the world that true freedom and fulfillment are found in commitment to God's purposes.

As a society, the 1980s left us with a stark lesson: the deconstruction of family values not only affects the home but erodes the very foundation of culture and spirituality. To restore these values, we must begin within the family, cultivating relationships based on love, respect, and mutual responsibility while rejecting cultural narratives that distort God's design.

The 1980s remind us of the importance of standing firm in biblical truth, even in the midst of a hostile cultural landscape. The task is challenging, but as 2 Corinthians 10:5 says: "We demolish arguments and every pretension that sets itself up against the knowledge of God, and we take captive every thought to make it obedient to Christ." This exhortation calls us to counter ideologies that seek to fragment eternal values and replace them with narratives of relativism and individualism.

1990'S

Masculinity in Crisis
and Commitment-Free Relationships

*"Husbands, love your wives,
just as Christ loved the church
and gave himself up for her."*
Ephesians 5:25

CHAPTER 5

1990s – Masculinity in Crisis and Commitment-Free Relationships

The Decade of Profound Cultural Change

The 1990s marked a radical shift in cultural dynamics, driven by globalization, the expansion of entertainment, and technological innovations such as the internet and video games. This decade brought with it an identity crisis for masculinity, a rise in radical feminism, and profound changes in human relationships. While cinema and television explored and legitimized new narratives, traditional structures, especially the family, experienced a silent but constant breakdown.

Masculinity in Crisis: Fragmentation and Search for Purpose

With the release of films like Fight Club (1999), a growing crisis in the perception of masculinity was exposed. The figure of the man, previously seen as a leader and provider, became a symbol of confusion and alienation. Tyler Durden, the protagonist of Fight Club, embodies the internal struggle of men trapped in a world that no longer values their role in the family or society. His search for purpose, though distorted, reflects the impact of consumerism and the disconnection from transcendent values.

This portrayal of masculinity echoed a cultural shift in a society that had ceased to view men as protectors and leaders. From a biblical perspective, Ephesians 5:25 highlights the sacrificial role of the husband as the leader in the home: "Husbands, love your wives, just as Christ loved the church." This ideal stood in stark contrast to the cultural messages describing men as irrelevant figures or individuals in constant internal conflict.

Radical Feminism: From the Fight for Equality to the Rejection of God's Design

Films such as Thelma & Louise (1991) offered a powerful narrative about women breaking free from patriarchal constraints. The protagonists, victims of abuse and oppression, choose a path of rebellion and self-discovery. While the film celebrated female freedom, it also depicted men as oppressors and family relationships as a trap.

This form of radical feminism rejected biblical principles that present women as a suitable and complementary helper, rather than a figure in conflict with men (Genesis 2:18). Proverbs 31:10-11 describes the virtuous woman as strong and wise, but 1990s cinema offered a distorted portrayal of this strength, promoting independence at the expense of family commitment.

Commitment-Free Relationships: A Generation of Individualism

Cinema and television also contributed to the normalization of commitment-free relationships. Films like Clueless (1995) and 10 Things I Hate About You (1999) glorified the exploration of adolescent identities and fleeting romantic relationships. These narratives transformed the concept of love, replacing sacrificial commitment with immediate gratification and convenience.

God's design for marriage, based on faithfulness and spiritual unity, is clearly outlined in Matthew 19:6: "So they are no longer two, but one flesh. Therefore, what God has joined together, let no one separate." However, these cultural representations promoted transactional and short-lived relationships, further weakening family values.

Entertainment as Refuge and Family Fragmentation

Technological advancements and the proliferation of media content transformed entertainment into an individualized refuge. Shows like Friends and The Simpsons offered alternative models of community, replacing family relationships with dynamics of friendship or humorous dysfunction. These representations not only reflected but also reinforced increasingly pronounced family fragmentation.

The Bible presents the family as God's design, the nucleus of moral and spiritual formation (Colossians 3:18-21). However, 1990s culture promoted a narrative that celebrated individuality and reduced the role of the family to an option rather than a social foundation.

A Legacy of Fragmentation and Self-Satisfaction

The 1990s solidified cultural changes that redefined masculinity, feminism, and human relationships. While cinema and television offered a narrative of independence and self-satisfaction, the traditional values of commitment and community eroded.

The legacy of this decade continues to resonate today, challenging those who seek to live according to God's design. Ephesians 4:3 exhorts us to maintain the unity of the Spirit through the bond of peace, reminding us that true purpose and fulfillment are found only in commitment to God's plan. The work of restoring these values begins at home, cultivating relationships based on love, respect, and mutual responsibility while resisting cultural narratives that promote self-satisfaction at the expense of God's design

2000'S

Reproductive Choices
and LGBTQ+ Visibility in the Digital Age

"Train up a child in the way he should go; even when he is old he will not depart from it."
Proverbs 22:6

CHAPTER 6

2000s – Reproductive Choices and LGBTQ+ Visibility in the Digital Age

The Digital Era and Its Impact on the Family

The 2000s marked an irreversible shift in family and social dynamics, driven by technological explosion and cultural globalization. High-speed internet, mobile devices, and emerging social networks like MySpace (2003) and Facebook (2004) redefined how people interacted, learned, and shared values. Although these technologies opened new opportunities for connection, they also fragmented family interaction, replacing shared activities with individualized experiences in front of screens.

The home, once a place of communion and moral formation, transformed into a space where each member consumed digital content in isolation. This phenomenon contrasted with biblical principles emphasizing shared family time as essential for the transmission of values: "These commandments that I give you today are to be on your hearts.

Impress them on your children. Talk about them when you sit at home and when you walk along the road" (Deuteronomy 6:6-7). However, the growing dependence on digital platforms eroded this model, promoting virtual hyperconnection at the expense of family bonds.

Two emblematic films of this decade, Juno (2007) and Brokeback Mountain (2005), captured the tensions of this cultural transformation, exploring themes like abortion, LGBTQ+ relationships, and the redefinition of marriage. These narratives, amplified by social media, not only reflected a change in values but actively promoted it, normalizing ideologies contrary to the biblical design of the family.

Juno (2007): Reproductive Autonomy and the Redefinition of Motherhood

The film Juno, directed by Jason Reitman, addresses teenage pregnancy from a contemporary perspective. Juno, the protagonist, chooses to give her child up for adoption, presenting a narrative that seemingly promotes life but also normalizes abortion as a legitimate option within the spectrum of reproductive choices. While the film avoids an openly pro-abortion stance, its emphasis on individual autonomy reinforces the idea that life in the womb is subject to the circumstances and desires of the mother.

This cultural approach contradicts the biblical principle that life is a sacred gift from God, not a human decision. "For you created my inmost being; you knit me together in my mother's womb" (Psalm 139:13). However, Juno reflects a culture beginning to view motherhood as an optional burden and life as negotiable, promoting a dangerous moral relativism.

The influence of the film was amplified on digital platforms such as YouTube and blogs, where debates on reproductive autonomy consolidated its cultural impact. This media environment helped spread the idea that decisions about life and motherhood should be governed by individual well-being, ignoring the moral and spiritual significance of giving life.

Brokeback Mountain (2005): The Redefinition of Marriage

While Juno tackled reproductive choices, Brokeback Mountain, directed by Ang Lee, directly challenged traditional notions of marriage. The love story between two men in a conservative, rural context sought to humanize and normalize LGBTQ+ relationships as a legitimate form of love, detaching them from God's design for the family. The emotionally impactful film appealed to the viewer's empathy, becoming a cultural catalyst for global acceptance of sexual diversity.

The success of Brokeback Mountain not only reflected but amplified a cultural narrative aimed at redefining marriage. From a biblical perspective, marriage is a covenant between a man and a woman, designed by God to reflect His relationship with His church: "That is why a man leaves his father and mother and is united to his wife, and they become one flesh" (Genesis 2:24). The film's narrative contradicted this design, promoting a model of relationships that prioritized individual authenticity over God's principles.

The Cultural Legacy of the 2000s

The decade of the 2000s marked a profound transformation in the perception of family, life, and marriage. Films like Juno and Brokeback Mountain, along with the expansion of social media, solidified narratives that challenged God's design for life and human relationships.

To counteract these influences, it is imperative for Christian families to reclaim the value of intergenerational teaching and reinforce biblical truth in their homes. "These commandments that I give you today are to be on your hearts; impress them on your children" (Deuteronomy 6:6-7). Only by affirming the sanctity of life, the importance of marriage, and the central role of the family in society can we resist the cultural forces seeking to erase God's eternal values.

The family remains the most powerful bulwark against moral fragmentation. In a hyperconnected but emotionally disconnected world, biblical teaching offers a clear and hopeful vision: "Then you will know the truth, and the truth will set you free" (John 8:32).

The Rise of Intersectional Feminism and the Challenge to Natural Order

"For we cannot do anything against the truth, but only for the truth."
2 Corinthians 13:8

CHAPTER 7

2010s – The Rise of Intersectional Feminism and the Challenge to Natural Order

Introduction to Intersectional Feminism and the Culture of Immediacy

The 2010s witnessed the consolidation of intersectional feminism as an influential cultural movement that transformed how society addresses issues of gender, race, oppression, and social justice. This approach, which sought to integrate multiple perspectives on inequality, challenged traditional structures and proposed a new narrative about identity and power. At the same time, the advancement of social media platforms like Instagram and Twitter promoted a culture of immediacy and external validation that amplified these ideas, fostering global debates and shaping cultural perceptions.

However, this shift also brought significant challenges to traditional family values and morality. Social media not only accelerated the dissemination of emerging ideologies but also fragmented time and family relationships, replacing personal connection with virtual interactions. This environment contrasted with the biblical design of the family as a space for communion and the transmission of values, as established in Psalm 78:5-6: "He decreed statutes for Jacob and established the law in Israel, which he commanded our ancestors to teach their children, so the next generation would know them, even the children yet to be born, and they in turn would tell their children."

In this context, cultural works such as The Handmaid's Tale (2017) and Moonlight (2016) became symbols of the era, reflecting and promoting narratives that challenged God's design for natural order and the family.

The Handmaid's Tale (2017): Dystopia and a Narrative of Oppression

Based on Margaret Atwood's novel, The Handmaid's Tale became a cultural phenomenon and a reference point for intersectional feminism. Set in a theocratic dystopia, the series depicts women subjected to an oppressive regime that reduces them to their reproductive roles. This narrative resonated strongly in the context of feminist movements of the decade, such as #MeToo, and was used as a symbol against patriarchy and systemic oppression.

However, the cultural interpretation of The Handmaid's Tale misrepresented biblical principles on marriage and family. While the series portrays these ideas as tools of oppression, the biblical perspective presents the home and marriage as spaces of love, unity, and complementarity. Ephesians 5:22-23 explains clearly: "Wives, submit yourselves to your own husbands as you do to the Lord. For the husband is the head of the wife as Christ is the head of the church." This passage does not advocate subjugation but sacrificial leadership and mutual love, reflecting the relationship between Christ and His church.

Through social media, The Handmaid's Tale amplified its influence by promoting a narrative that challenged God's design but also revealed a constant search for meaning and justice in a society rejecting eternal values.

Moonlight (2016): Identity, Race, and Family

In contrast, Moonlight, directed by Barry Jenkins, explored the intersection of race, poverty, and sexual orientation, narrating the story of a young African American seeking his identity in a hostile environment. The film, acclaimed for its sensitivity, questioned traditional structures by presenting a narrative where family relationships and traditional values were secondary to the personal search for meaning.

While powerful in its message, Moonlight reflects a disconnect from the biblical principle that the family is the primary space for formation and support. Proverbs 22:6 teaches: "Start children off on the way they should go, and even when they are old they will not turn from it." However, the film portrays characters seeking belonging and purpose outside the home, in an environment where moral and cultural norms are fluid.

The narrative of Moonlight was also amplified through digital platforms, becoming a symbol of resistance to traditional structures and promoting new forms of identity that challenged God's design.

The Impact of Intersectional Feminism on the Family

Intersectional feminism, along with the cultural narratives of The Handmaid's Tale and Moonlight, transformed perceptions of family and gender roles during the 2010s. These narratives portrayed the nuclear family as an oppressive institution and questioned traditional values, promoting a vision in which identity and justice were found outside God's design.

However, the Bible presents the family as God's design, intended to reflect His love and purpose. Psalm 128:3-4 describes: "Your wife will be like a fruitful vine within your house; your children will be like olive shoots around your table." This model not only ensures stability but also provides a moral and spiritual legacy that transcends generations.

Social platforms played a crucial role in this cultural shift, promoting individualism and intersectional narratives at the expense of family values. While these digital tools facilitated global communication, they also fragmented family relationships and prioritized external validation over deep connections.

Restoring the Family Amid Fragmentation

The 2010s marked a profound shift in perceptions of family, gender, and identity. Narratives such as those in The Handmaid's Tale and Moonlight, along with the rise of intersectional feminism, challenged traditional values and promoted ideologies that further fragmented the family unit.

However, God's truth remains unchanging in the face of these cultural challenges. The family, as designed by God, is not an oppressive construct but a reflection of His love and eternal purpose. Restoring this design requires renewed commitment to biblical principles and clear teaching that affirms the truth.

2 Corinthians 13:8 tells us: "For we cannot do anything against the truth, but only for the truth." This truth must be the anchor for those who seek to resist cultural currents that blur eternal values and fragment the home.

The call to action is clear: to reaffirm the original design of the family as a space for love, sacrifice, and the transmission of values, and to use digital platforms as tools for promoting truth and restoration. In the face of a culture seeking to redefine the natural order, the family remains the strongest bulwark against moral and spiritual fragmentation.

20 20's

The Challenging Truth - Restoring the Family in a Fragmented World

"Jesus Christ is the same yesterday and today and forever."
Hebrews 13:8

CHAPTER 8

2020s – The Challenging Truth: Restoring the Family in a Fragmented World

The Radicalization of Ideologies and Cultural Impact on the Family

The 2020s have intensified the deconstruction of fundamental truths about gender and family, bringing us into an era of redefinition where traditional structures are perceived as outdated and restrictive. Cinema, digital platforms, and social media have become cultural weapons that promote gender fluidity, the redefinition of relationships, and extreme individualism, all in the name of progress and inclusion. However, from a Christian perspective, these changes do not represent progress but a rupture with God's perfect design for humanity.

Gender Fluidity as a Central Narrative

Films such as Barbie (2023) and Everything Everywhere All at Once (2022) are emblematic examples of how the cultural industry has adopted and promoted gender fluidity as a fundamental principle. In Barbie, the narrative focuses on the search for individual identity outside traditional structures, presenting a critique of patriarchy that, while addressing real issues, also promotes a view of femininity and masculinity detached from God's purpose.

In contrast, Everything Everywhere All at Once offers a chaotic, multidimensional narrative symbolizing the fragmentation of human identity and relationships. Through its protagonist, the film suggests that meaning and belonging must be sought outside family structures, adapting to personal circumstances and desires. This approach contradicts God's design, which presents the family as a nucleus of stability, love, and eternal purpose (Ephesians 5:23-25).

Cinema as a Tool of Deconstruction

The impact of these productions is not limited to cinemas. Social media platforms like TikTok, Instagram, and Twitter have amplified these narratives, turning the films into cultural symbols of resistance and redefinition. However, this fluid and relativistic narrative contrasts with biblical teachings that proclaim truth as absolute and unchanging, as stated in Psalm 119:160: "The sum of your word is truth, and every one of your righteous rules endures forever."

The deconstruction promoted by these narratives is not an isolated phenomenon, but part of a broader process designed to dismantle fundamental principles of family and morality. This is evident in the growing acceptance of concepts like "free love," the redefinition of motherhood and fatherhood, and the normalization of fluid identities that reject God's design.

Impact on Emerging Generations

The youth of this generation have been particularly influenced by these narratives, adopting as normal ideas that would have been unthinkable years ago. Digital platforms not only serve as sources of entertainment but also as primary educators of ideological values, where biblical principles are increasingly displaced by relativistic perspectives.

However, the Bible establishes the family as the primary space for the transmission of values and spiritual formation, as mentioned in Deuteronomy 4:9: "Only be careful, and watch yourselves closely so that you do not forget the things your eyes have seen or let them fade from your heart as long as you live. Teach them to your children and to their children after them." This contrast between eternal values and cultural narratives underscores the urgency of reaffirming God's design in a world struggling to find meaning outside His truth.

The Biblical Response: Restoration and Truth

In light of this landscape, it is essential for believers not only to recognize the cultural threat but also to respond with clarity and conviction. The family, as God's design, is not an arbitrary construct but a reflection of the love and unity God desires for His creation. Colossians 3:14-15 reminds us that Christ's love and peace should govern our relationships: "And over all these virtues put on love, which binds them all together in perfect unity. Let the peace of Christ rule in your hearts."

Restoring the family as the nucleus of society begins with a renewed commitment to biblical principles. This involves not only teaching the truth but also living it in a way that future generations can see its relevance and transformative power. The clear instruction of Deuteronomy 6:6-7 emphasizes the importance of passing down God's commandments to children, ensuring His truth remains at the center of our lives and relationships.

The Family as a Bulwark of Truth

The cultural challenges of the 2020s are immense but not insurmountable. In a world that glorifies fluidity and relativism, God's truth remains an unshakable anchor for those who trust in His design. As Hebrews 13:8 declares: "Jesus Christ is the same yesterday, today, and forever." This unchanging foundation provides hope for families seeking to remain faithful in the midst of a hostile environment.

Restoring the family requires intentional action and a commitment to biblical truth. By proclaiming and living this truth, believers can be a light in a world filled with confusion, reminding others that the family, as God designed it, remains the strongest refuge against ideologies that seek to fragment it.

The Role of Men
and Women in God's Design

*"So God created mankind in his
own image, in the image of
God he created them; male and
female he created them."*
Genesis 1:27

CHAPTER 9

The Role of Men and Women in God's Design

The Family as God's Design

The family, from its inception in Eden, is the fundamental institution created by God to reflect His love, character, and purpose for humanity. In a culture that increasingly blurs the roles and responsibilities of genders, restoring God's design is not only urgent but vital. The contemporary confusion surrounding the roles of men and women in the family is the result of a profound disconnection from the truth of Scripture and God's perfect plan.

The Original Design: Equality in Value, Difference in Purpose

The creation of man and woman described in Genesis 1:27-28 highlights their complementarity: "So God created mankind in his own image, in the image of God he created them; male and female he created them. God blessed them and said to them, 'Be fruitful and increase in number; fill the earth and subdue it.'" This statement emphasizes that both were created equal in dignity and value, but with roles designed to complement each other in unity.

The Hebrew word ezer, used in Genesis 2:18 to describe the woman as a "helper suitable," does not denote inferiority. On the contrary, the term appears in Scripture in direct reference to God Himself, as in Psalm 33:20: "We wait in hope for the Lord; he is our help and our shield." This implies that the woman's role is essential, significant, and vital in the joint mission of co-governing creation and establishing God's order on earth.

However, modern cultural narratives have replaced this vision with ideologies that promote competition instead of collaboration. Influences like gender ideology and radical feminist movements have attempted to redefine gender roles as oppressive structures, ignoring God's original design.

The Man: Leadership in Service and Sacrifice

In Ephesians 5:25, Paul describes God's standard for husbands: "Husbands, love your wives, just as Christ loved the church and gave himself up for her." This model of leadership is not based on domination but on sacrifice and service. The husband is called to lead his home with love, following the example of Christ.

In contrast, contemporary culture has promoted a distorted image of men, oscillating between "toxic masculinity" and a loss of identity. Films like Fight Club (1999) reflect this crisis by portraying men as trapped between social pressures and emotional disconnection. However, true male leadership is not found in brute strength or self-sufficiency but in loving sacrifice that builds and protects the family.

The Woman: A Pillar of Strength and Nurturing

The biblical model of women, described in Proverbs 31, highlights her role as a pillar of strength, wisdom, and nurturing in the home and society: "She considers a field and buys it; out of her earnings, she plants a vineyard." This passage contrasts with modern narratives that present motherhood and marriage as limitations to personal fulfillment. Films like Thelma & Louise (1991) and Nine to Five (1980) have promoted the idea that absolute independence is the ultimate goal, disconnecting it from God's purpose.

The biblical design, however, portrays women as equal partners in value and fundamental to the family's mission. This balance challenges both passive dependence and radical autonomy, offering a model that celebrates female strength in unity with men.

Complementarity: A Perfect Design

God's design does not foster competition between genders but collaboration. When men and women fulfill their biblical roles, they reflect the harmony and unity that strengthen the family and the community. However, Marxist narratives, like those of Antonio Gramsci, have sought to redefine these relationships, promoting the idea that the family is a social construct meant to perpetuate oppression.

The Bible offers a radically different perspective. In Colossians 3:18-21, Paul describes God's model for family relationships, emphasizing the importance of authority and mutual love: "Children, obey your parents in everything, for this pleases the Lord. Fathers, do not embitter your children, or they will become discouraged."

Strategies for Restoring God's Design

1. Biblical Education: Teaching roles and responsibilities from a biblical perspective must be a priority in churches and Christian communities.
2. Family Discipleship: Couples must be discipled to live according to the biblical model of love and collaboration, strengthening their marriages.
3. Open Communication: Husbands and wives must work together to address modern challenges and build homes that reflect God's truth.

4. Visible Role Models: Spiritual leaders should exemplify how to live out God's design in the family, inspiring others to follow their example.

5. Preparing the Next Generation: Teach young people to value and prepare for their future roles in the family from a biblical perspective.

Restoring God's Order

The family is the nucleus where character is formed, values are cultivated, and unconditional love is experienced. In an increasingly fragmented world, Christians are called to be agents of restoration. The prophet Malachi foretold this mission in Malachi 4:5-6: "He will turn the hearts of the parents to their children, and the hearts of the children to their parents."

This movement of reconciliation, symbolized by the "Spirit of Elijah," is essential in the last days. As families align with God's design, they will reflect His glory and restore humanity's original purpose. The spiritual and moral restoration of the family is not only a response to current challenges but also preparation for the Lord's return and the establishment of His eternal kingdom.

Recovering
the Value of the Family

*"Unless the Lord builds the
house, the builders labor in
vain."*
Psalm 127:1

CHAPTER 10

Recovering the Value of the Family

God's Design Amid Contemporary Crisis

The family, instituted by God as the essential nucleus of society, has been the target of cultural and spiritual attacks since the beginning of humanity. Over the decades, the roles, values, and purposes of God for the home have been distorted, eroding the foundations that sustain both individuals and communities. However, God's design for the family is perfect and unchanging—a model that, when followed, brings fulfillment, order, and blessing.

The restoration of the family is not only possible but essential. This chapter offers an in-depth analysis of how to rediscover the eternal purpose of the family, confront cultural challenges, and foster homes that reflect the character of Christ.

The Family as God's Design: An Eternal Foundation

From the very beginning, God established the family as a reflection of His character and purpose for humanity. Genesis 1:27-28 states: "So God created mankind in his own image... male and female he created them. God blessed them and said to them, 'Be fruitful and increase in number; fill the earth and subdue it.'" This command revealed the purpose of the family as a space for growth, reproduction, and governance on earth under God's direction, within God's order.

Marriage, as the foundation of the family, is not a social construct but a sacred institution designed to reflect the union between Christ and His church (Ephesians 5:31-32). This model establishes that men and women have complementary roles, called to work together to fulfill God's mission on earth.

In a world that celebrates individual autonomy and moral relativism, the family has been degraded to an optional construct, disconnected from its eternal purpose. Yet the Scriptures remind us in Psalm 127:1: "Unless the Lord builds the house, the builders labor in vain." The family, far from being a transient concept, is a pillar of God's kingdom.

Contemporary Challenges: Fragmentation and Root-lessness

Modern culture has introduced ideologies and narratives that attack the original design of the family. Among these challenges are:

1. The Exaltation of Individualism: Films and television series have promoted personal fulfillment as incompatible with family sacrifice and commitment. Works like Marriage Story (2019) depict the tension between individual dreams and marital union, perpetuating the idea that marriage can be discarded if it obstructs "personal happiness."

2. The Impact of Technology and Entertainment: Digital hyperconnectivity has replaced deep family interactions with superficial content and consumerism. Social media platforms like Instagram and TikTok foster a sense of external validation, drawing young people away from family and spiritual values.

3. The Deconstruction of Gender Roles: Influenced by postmodern ideologies, cultural narratives have erased distinctions between male and female roles, leading to an identity crisis for both men and women. However, the Bible affirms in 1 Corinthians 11:3: "But I want you to realize that the head of every man is Christ, and the head of the woman is man, and the head of Christ is God."

These challenges are not cultural accidents; they are deliberate tools aimed at uprooting families from God's purpose, plunging society into confusion and fragmentation.

Strategies for the Restoration of the Family

The church is called to be an agent of transformation in restoring the biblical model of the family. This process begins with teaching and practicing biblical principles, addressing contemporary challenges with intentionality and truth.

1. Generational Reconciliation: Restoring relationships between parents and children is essential for family unity. Malachi 4:6 promises: "He will turn the hearts of the parents to their children, and the hearts of the children to their parents." This involves dedicating time to strengthening family bonds through open communication, shared time, and collective prayer.

2. Strengthening Family Discipleship: Parents are the primary disciplers of their children. Deuteronomy 6:6-7 instructs: "These commandments that I give you today are to be on your hearts. Impress them on your children." This intentional teaching model not only strengthens individual faith but also prepares future generations to be light in a dark world.

3. Defending the Biblical Model: Believers must be equipped to confront cultural narratives that trivialize the family and Christian values. This includes

defending biblical truth with love and grace, proclaiming that the family is God's design and cannot be substituted.

4. Living Example in Christian Homes: Christian homes must be a testimony to the gospel. Matthew 5:16 exhorts: "Let your light shine before others, that they may see your good deeds and glorify your Father in heaven." This means modeling love, respect, and forgiveness within the family, demonstrating to the world the transformative power of Christ.

Practical Strategies for Strengthening Families

1. Establish Spiritual Priorities: Set aside daily time for family prayer and Bible reading.
2. Disconnect from Technology: Dedicate time free from devices to foster communication and shared activities.
3. Engage in Community Service: Focus the family on serving others as a practical expression of Christ's love.
4. Celebrate Family Unity: Establish traditions and special moments that reinforce family bonds.

The Church as an Agent of Restoration

The church must be a refuge and a center for equipping families. Hebrews 10:24-25 reads: "And let us consider how we may spur one another on toward love and good deeds, not giving up meeting together." In this context, churches can implement:

1. Family Support Ministries: Discipleship groups for couples, parenting classes, and intergenerational mentorship programs.
2. Preaching and Teaching Centered on Family: Equip believers with biblical tools to face modern challenges.
3. Creating Supportive Communities: Spaces where families can share, learn, and build each other up.

The Family as a Testimony of God's Kingdom

A family that lives according to God's design is a powerful testimony in a broken world. Such families not only reflect the character of Christ but also serve as beacons of hope and reconciliation. Romans 12:2 reminds us: "Do not conform to the pattern of this world but be transformed by the renewing of your mind."

Restoring the family is a prophetic call to prepare the way for the Lord. In a world searching for meaning, the family remains a tangible reminder that purpose, truth, and unconditional love are found in God's eternal design. By embracing this model, Christian families will not only live in fullness but also guide others toward the hope that is found only in Christ.

A Path to Spiritual and Moral Restoration

"If my people, who are called by my name, will humble themselves and pray and seek my face and turn from their wicked ways, then I will hear from heaven."
2 Chronicles 7:14

CHAPTER 11

A Path to Spiritual and Moral Restoration

A Call to Face the Cultural Crisis

The family, as an institution designed by God, has been under constant attack over the decades. From the exaltation of individualism to the deconstruction of gender roles, cinema, television, and digital platforms have played a key role in shaping perceptions that erode biblical values. Despite this, the battle is not lost. Spiritual and moral restoration offers an opportunity for believers to live counter-culturally and reflect God's design in a broken world.

The Apostle Paul reminds us of the spiritual nature of this struggle in Ephesians 6:12: "For our struggle is not against flesh and blood, but against the rulers, against the authorities, against the powers of this dark world." This means that restoring family values cannot be achieved solely through social arguments or cultural resistance but with spiritual weapons founded on the Word of God.

Reflection on Cultural Influence

The power of cinema and television to shape mindsets cannot be underestimated. Over decades of influence, these tools have promoted values that redefine key concepts such as family, love, and purpose. However, the Word of God warns against uncritically adopting the world's narratives. Romans 12:2 exhorts: "Do not conform to the pattern of this world but be transformed by the renewing of your mind."

Contemporary culture has normalized behaviors and beliefs that contradict God's design. For instance, films have depicted marriage as an outdated institution and family as a restrictive construct. Instead of reflecting Christ's sacrificial love and eternal commitment, many narratives have promoted self-gratification as the highest value.

Spiritual Restoration: The Path to Family Unity

The starting point for restoring the family is the transformation of the individual. Only a heart surrendered to Christ can model biblical principles within the home. 2 Chronicles 7:14 says, "If my people, who are called by my name, will humble themselves and pray and seek my face and turn from their wicked ways, then I will hear from heaven, and I will forgive their sin and will heal their land."

Key steps toward restoration:

1. Genuine Repentance: Recognizing and rejecting cultural influences that have distorted our understanding of the family and its roles. 1 John 1:9 assures: "If we confess our sins, he is faithful and just and will forgive us our sins and purify us from all unrighteousness."

2. Dependence on the Holy Spirit: Restoration is not a human effort but a work of God. Jesus promised in John 14:26 that the Holy Spirit will teach us all things and remind us of God's truth.

3. Intentional Discipleship: Parents must be the primary spiritual guides of their children, forming a "domestic church" where the values of God's Kingdom are lived out. Deuteronomy 6:6-7 underscores the importance of diligently teaching the Word to the next generations.

The Role of the Church in Moral Restoration

The church, as the community of God's people, has a vital role in defending the family. Beyond being a spiritual refuge, it must act as an equipping center for families, preparing them to face cultural challenges with truth and love.

Essential strategies for the church:

1. Faithful and Relevant Preaching: The proclamation of the Word must confront cultural narratives and equip believers with a solid biblical worldview. Hebrews 4:12 affirms that the Word is alive and active, able to judge the thoughts and attitudes of the heart.

2. Creating Supportive Communities: Spaces where families can share their struggles and successes, building one another up. Galatians 6:2 instructs: "Carry each other's burdens, and in this way, you will fulfill the law of Christ."

3. Intergenerational Mentorship: Connecting older generations with younger ones to pass on wisdom and strengthen community bonds. Titus 2:3-5 exhorts older women to teach the younger ones to love their husbands and children.

Believers as Light in the Darkness

In a world that promotes confusion and fragmentation, Christians are called to be salt and light. Matthew 5:16 says: "Let your light shine before others, that they may see your good deeds and glorify your Father in heaven." This call is not optional but an unavoidable mission for those redeemed by Christ.

How believers can impact culture:

1. Modeling God's Design: Every Christian home should be an example of love, forgiveness, and service, showcasing the beauty of God's design to the world.
2. Engaging in the Public Sphere: Believers must participate in creating content that reflects Kingdom values, from cinema and literature to social media.
3. Educating with Discernment: Equipping young people with biblical tools to recognize and resist cultural lies.

The Family: The Heart of Cultural Redemption

God designed the family not only as a space of love and unity but as a living testimony of His relationship with His people. Restoring families is essential for the cultural and spiritual redemption of society. Joshua 24:15 declares: "But as for me and my household, we will serve the Lord," a reminder that every Christian home has an eternal impact.

Malachi 4:6 prophesies the reconciliation between parents and children as a sign of the promised restoration: "He will turn the hearts of the parents to their children, and the hearts of the children to their parents." This reconciliation not only strengthens individual relationships but also lays the groundwork for a broader transformation in humanity.

An Urgent Call to Action

Spiritual and moral restoration is not just an ideal but an urgent necessity in a world that has lost its anchor in truth. From small acts of family prayer to active participation in the church and culture, every effort matters in building a collective testimony that glorifies God.

Isaiah 58:12 says: "Your people will rebuild the ancient ruins and will raise up the age-old foundations; you will be called Repairer of Broken Walls, Restorer of Streets with Dwellings." This call is both individual and collective: a challenge to restore what the world has tried to destroy and to build a culture that reflects the Kingdom of God.

With Christ's help, believers can resist cultural lies, strengthen their families, and be agents of hope in a world yearning for redemption. The family, as God's design, is the means through which His light shines most brightly in the midst of cultural darkness.

The Christian Worldview as the Foundation for Restoration

"For the Lord gives wisdom; from his mouth come knowledge and understanding."
Proverbs 2:6

CHAPTER 12

The Christian Worldview as the Foundation for Restoration

The Restorative Power of the Christian Worldview

Since its origin, Christianity has served as a moral and spiritual anchor during times of chaos and decline. Its worldview, grounded in the Word of God, answers humanity's deepest questions: Who are we? What is our purpose? What defines our values? The Bible reminds us that we were created in God's image (Genesis 1:27) and that every social structure must reflect God's design. Therefore, the restoration of society requires a deliberate and conscious return to God's eternal principles.

The Challenge of Contemporary Culture

Modern culture's departure from its Christian roots has led to ethical and moral fragmentation. Today, personal autonomy is celebrated as the greatest good, while absolute values are dismissed as outdated. 2 Timothy 3:1-5 warns: "But mark this: There will be terrible times in the last days. People will be lovers of themselves, lovers of money, boastful, proud, abusive..." This diagnosis accurately describes a society that has lost its sense of collective responsibility.

The consequences of this disconnection are clear: the dissolution of the family, the exaltation of moral relativism, and the redefinition of human identity. However, the Christian worldview, when lived sincerely, has the power to transform both the individual and society. Psalm 127:1 says: "Unless the Lord builds the house, the builders labor in vain."

The Christian as an Agent of Transformation

Jesus called His disciples to be "the salt of the earth" and "the light of the world" (Matthew 5:13-16). These metaphors highlight believers' active role in preserving morality and illuminating eternal truths. Salt preserves against corruption, while light exposes and corrects darkness.

Spheres of Influence

1. Education: Christians must actively participate in shaping future generations, imparting biblical principles that counter secular philosophies.
2. Art and Culture: Cinema, music, and literature can be powerful tools to communicate Kingdom values.
3. Politics and Economy: Engaging in the public sphere with integrity, seeking justice and the common good.

The Christian presence should not be merely decorative. The principles of God's Kingdom are profoundly relevant to all aspects of human life. Colossians 3:17 exhorts: "And whatever you do, whether in word or deed, do it all in the name of the Lord Jesus."

Sacrificial Love as the Driving Force of Restoration

Christianity is distinguished by its emphasis on sacrificial love, exemplified on the cross of Christ (John 15:13). This love transforms not only individuals but also communities. In a world dominated by competition and division, love that seeks the welfare of others is a powerful tool for reconciliation.

When Christian families live out this love, they reflect God's design and offer an alternative model to cultural fragmentation. Ephesians 4:2-3 says: "Be completely humble and gentle; be patient, bearing with one another in love. Make every effort to keep the unity of the Spirit through the bond of peace."

The Church as a Community of Hope

The church, as the body of Christ (1 Corinthians 12:27), has a fundamental role in social restoration. In a time when many institutions have lost credibility, the church must be a refuge of truth, comfort, and action.

Key Roles of the Church

1. Discipleship: Equipping believers to face cultural challenges with a solid biblical worldview. 2 Timothy 2:2 calls for passing on teaching to "reliable people who will also be qualified to teach others."
2. Authentic Fellowship: Creating spaces where people can find mutual support and grow spiritually. Hebrews 10:24-25 exhorts believers not to forsake meeting together but to encourage one another.
3. Social Action: Serving local communities, demonstrating Christ's love through practical deeds.

The Power of Collective Testimony

Throughout history, Christians have transformed cultures by living in community according to Kingdom principles. From the early believers in the Roman Empire to movements like abolitionism and social reform, collective testimony has demonstrated the impact of faith in action.

Today, Christian families have the opportunity to be a living testimony of reconciliation and hope in a broken world. Acts 4:32 describes the early church: "All the believers were one in heart and mind." This model remains relevant, showing that unity in Christ has a transformative impact.

A Vision of Restoration and Hope

Although the challenges are significant, the Christian worldview offers unwavering hope. It is not merely about resisting evil but actively participating in God's redemptive work. Isaiah 61:4 proclaims: "They will rebuild the ancient ruins and restore the places long devastated; they will renew the ruined cities that have been devastated for generations."

This vision of restoration is rooted in the promise that God is working all things for the good of those who love Him (Romans 8:28). By committing to this calling, we not only help build a society that honors God but also bear witness to His eternal Kingdom.

The Call to Be Bearers of Light

In a world struggling to find purpose and meaning, Christians are called to be agents of transformation. The family, the church, and the community can become beacons of hope when aligned with God's design.

Micah 6:8 summarizes this call: "He has shown you, O mortal, what is good. And what does the Lord require of you? To act justly and to love mercy and to walk humbly with your God." With faith, humility, and deliberate action, believers can counter contemporary culture and build a society that reflects God's love and truth.

Restoration is not merely an ideal; it is a reality that manifests when God's people live according to His Word. In this mission, we find not only our purpose but also the eternal glory of the One who called us out of darkness into His marvelous light. 1 Peter 2:9 reminds us: "But you are a chosen people, a royal priesthood, a holy nation, God's special possession."

Living as Salt
and Light
in a Culture in Crisis

*"You are the salt of the earth; but
if the salt loses its flavor, how
shall it be seasoned?"*
Matthew 5:13

CHAPTER 13

Living as Salt and Light in a Culture in Crisis

Christ's Command: Be Salt and Light in the World

Jesus' call in Matthew 5:13-16 is not a theological suggestion; it is an urgent command that requires immediate action. In a world increasingly distanced from God's principles, Jesus reminds us that we are agents of preservation and transformation: "You are the salt of the earth... You are the light of the world." This message not only identifies us but also assigns us a mission: to preserve the truth, dispel darkness, and glorify God through our actions.

Being salt means halting the spiritual and moral decay threatening to dissolve society. It also means adding flavor to collective life with values like love, justice, and mercy. Being light, on the other hand, means shining with the clarity of biblical truth, exposing and confronting the darkness that dominates so many areas of our culture. Ephesians 5:8 exhorts: "For you were once darkness, but now you are light in the Lord. Live as children of light."

Not Conforming but Transforming

The apostle Paul challenges us in Romans 12:2: "Do not conform to the pattern of this world but be transformed by the renewing of your mind." Similarly, Ephesians 4:22-24 says: "You were taught, with regard to your former way of life, to put off your old self, which is being corrupted by its deceitful desires; to be made new in the attitude of your minds; and to put on the new self, created to be like God in true righteousness and holiness." This call is both a warning and an invitation. In an age where cultural conformity exerts overwhelming pressure, Christians must resist the temptation to align with dominant narratives and instead be agents of change.

Modern society, as analyzed by Antonio Gramsci, uses cultural hegemony to shape collective thought, often without people even realizing it. As Christians, we cannot ignore this reality. We must discern the ideologies attempting to divert us from God's design and present a solid, coherent alternative based on His Word. 2 Corinthians 10:5 declares: "We demolish arguments and every pretension that sets itself up against the knowledge of God, and we take captive every thought to make it obedient to Christ."

Forming Living and Discipling Communities

The book of Acts offers us a powerful model of how the early church lived out its faith in a hostile world. In Acts 2:42-

47, we find a church committed to teaching, fellowship, prayer, and action. These communities transformed their environment because they intentionally and practically lived out the principles of God's Kingdom.

Today, our churches must be more than spiritual refuges. They must become workshops of discipleship where believers are equipped to bring an active, visible faith to every area of life. This means:

Equipping believers to live out their faith in their homes, workplaces, and communities.

1. Modeling a Christian life that impacts and transforms spheres such as politics, education, art, and media.
2. Strengthening unity within the body of Christ so that our collective actions have a greater impact.
3. Philippians 1:27 urges us: "Whatever happens, conduct yourselves in a manner worthy of the gospel of Christ."

Making Tangible Change

Cultural transformation will not happen by accident. It requires intentionality, strategy, and action rooted in biblical truth.

1. Educate on cultural trends: Christians must understand the ideologies shaping our society. We need to

study them—not to imitate but to confront them with the truth of Scripture. 1 Peter 3:15 calls us to always "be prepared to give an answer... with gentleness and respect."

2. Create local and international support networks: Unity in the body of Christ is essential. Churches, communities, and leaders must collaborate to share resources and strategies that amplify our impact. Hebrews 10:24 exhorts: "And let us consider how we may spur one another on toward love and good deeds."

3. Produce truth-based content: Technology and media are powerful tools that must be redeemed for the Kingdom. It is time to create content that challenges cultural lies with truths that illuminate and restore. Psalm 96:3 declares: "Declare his glory among the nations, his marvelous deeds among all peoples."

4. Participate in places of influence: Christians must be present in decision-making and leadership spaces. From politics to education and the arts, it is necessary to bring Christ's light to where it is most needed. Proverbs 31:8-9 encourages: "Speak up for those who cannot speak for themselves... Speak up and judge fairly."

A Call to Committed Leadership

This challenge is not just for pastors and church leaders; it is for every believer. The responsibility of leading cultural change falls on all who have been redeemed by Christ. 2

Timothy 4:2 instructs: "Preach the word; be prepared in season and out of season."

Committed leadership must:

1. Inspire churches to step out of their comfort zones.
2. Equip congregations to live out their faith practically and trans formatively.
3. Foster a vision of impact that encompasses both local and global outreach.

Living as Lights in a Crooked Generation

In the midst of a darkened world, Christians are called to shine as lights. Philippians 2:15 reminds us to be "blameless and pure, children of God without fault in a warped and crooked generation." This testimony is achieved not only through words but through transformed lives that reflect Christ's love, truth, and power.

1. Be examples at home: The family is the first place where the Christian faith should be lived and modeled. Joshua 24:15 declares: "But as for me and my household, we will serve the Lord."
2. Impact communities: Through acts of love and justice, we can demonstrate the difference Christ makes in our lives. Micah 6:8 calls us to "act justly, love mercy, and walk humbly with your God."

3. Proclaim the gospel boldly: In a world that seeks to silence the truth, we must speak with conviction and love. Romans 1:16 proclaims: "For I am not ashamed of the gospel, because it is the power of God that brings salvation."

An Eternal Mission

The impact of our actions today will have eternal repercussions. If we remain faithful to Christ's call to be salt and light, we will see our communities, nations, and world begin to reflect God's Kingdom in tangible, redemptive ways. As 1 Corinthians 15:58 encourages: "Always give yourselves fully to the work of the Lord, because you know that your labor in the Lord is not in vain."

We are not alone in this mission. Jesus promised to be with us until the end of the age (Matthew 28:20). In Him and with the power of the Holy Spirit, we can face any challenge, restore our families, transform our cultures, and glorify His name in all we do.

Using Media to Spread the Truth

"Declare his glory among the nations, his marvelous deeds among all peoples."
Psalm 96:3

CHAPTER 14

Using Media to Spread the Truth

Redefining Media as Tools for God's Kingdom

In an era where mass media and digital platforms shape society's ideologies and values, Christians must embrace their responsibility as communicators of the truth. Media are not intrinsically good or bad; their value depends on the message they convey and the hands that wield them.

The apostle Paul reminds us in 2 Corinthians 10:4-5 that "the weapons we fight with are not the weapons of the world. On the contrary, they have divine power to demolish strongholds. We demolish arguments and every pretension that sets itself up against the knowledge of God." This passage calls us to use available tools, including media, to dismantle cultural lies and exalt the truth of Christ. The battle for minds and hearts is spiritual, and media serve as a key battleground in this conflict.

The Manufacture of Consent and Ideological Control

Cultural hegemony is consolidated through control of the media. This phenomenon, described by authors like Antonio Gramsci and Noam Chomsky, manipulates collective perceptions by continuously repeating narratives that ultimately become accepted as normal.

As Christians, we cannot be passive spectators in this cultural battle. We must discern the underlying ideologies and respond with creativity and biblical fidelity. 1 John 2:15-17 tells us: "Do not love the world or anything in the world. If anyone loves the world, love for the Father is not in them. For everything in the world—the lust of the flesh, the lust of the eyes, and the pride of life—comes not from the Father but from the world." We must refuse to passively accept dominant narratives and be prepared to offer an alternative rooted in God's truth.

Transforming Media into Tools of Truth

Access to digital platforms has democratized communication, opening a window of opportunity for believers to use these tools for the Kingdom. However, this requires intentionality, commitment, and excellence. Below are three key approaches to transforming media into tools of truth.

Producing Christ-Centered Content:

Creating audiovisual content that reflects biblical principles is essential. This includes films, documentaries, podcasts, web series, and other formats that communicate God's truth with quality and creativity. Examples like The Chosen demonstrate that it is possible to produce content with artistic excellence and spiritual depth.

Colossians 3:23 says: "Whatever you do, work at it with all your heart, as working for the Lord, not for human masters." This standard motivates us to pursue excellence in every project, understanding that our work is an offering to the Lord.

Educating in Media Discernment:

Mass consumption of information makes it urgent to teach congregations, especially young people, to critically analyze media messages. This includes identifying hidden agendas and evaluating content from a biblical perspective. Philippians 4:8 exhorts: "Finally, brothers and sisters, whatever is true, whatever is noble, whatever is right, whatever is pure... if anything is excellent or praiseworthy—think about such things." This serves as a guide to filter what we consume and focus on what builds us up.

Building Networks of Christian Communicators:

It is necessary to establish alliances among Christian communicators to amplify the gospel message. These networks can share resources, train leaders in communication, and support projects that impact culture. Ecclesiastes 4:9-10 highlights the importance of collaboration: "Two are better than one because they have a good return for their labor: If either of them falls down, one can help the other up." Working together enhances our impact on the world.

A Battle for Minds and Hearts

The battle for media transcends technology; it is a spiritual struggle for souls. As Ephesians 6:12 affirms: "For our struggle is not against flesh and blood, but against the rulers, against the authorities, against the powers of this dark world..." This understanding should motivate us to pray fervently for media and act courageously.

Commitment to Excellence and Truth

Using media for God's glory demands excellence. In a market saturated with content, our message must stand out not only for its substance but also for its quality. Proverbs 22:29 reminds us: "Do you see someone skilled in their work? They will serve before kings." Quality and dedication are tangible testimonies of our faith.

A Call to Action

Commitment to the truth begins with each of us. No matter how small our efforts may seem, we are all called to contribute. From sharing messages on social media to learning technical skills to support Christian projects, our actions can become powerful tools in God's hands. 1 Peter 4:10 exhorts: "Each of you should use whatever gift you have received to serve others, as faithful stewards of God's grace in its various forms."

Reflecting God's Glory on Every Screen

Screens are windows to the soul, and our responsibility as Christians is to fill them with light. Jesus said in Matthew 5:16: "Let your light shine before others, that they may see your good deeds and glorify your Father in heaven." If we take this command seriously, we will see how media can be transformed into instruments of spiritual and cultural restoration.

Final Proposal

We cannot wait for others to lead this change. You and I are called to be agents of transformation, bringing the gospel to every pixel and every word. Though the task is great, we trust that the Lord will guide and provide for us to fulfill this mission. 2 Timothy 1:7 assures: "For the Spirit God gave us does not make us timid, but gives us power, love, and self-discipline." With this confidence, let us move forward boldly to proclaim the truth in every corner of the digital world.

Preparing
the Next Generation:
Equipping Young People
to Transform Culture

"These commandments that I give you today are to be on your hearts. Impress them on your children."
Deuteronomy 6:6-7

CHAPTER 15

Preparing the Next Generation: Equipping Young People to Transform Culture

The Urgency of Holistic Formation

Today's youth face a cultural landscape deeply influenced by ideologies aimed at distorting God's truth. From social media to educational systems, dominant narratives promote relativism, instant gratification, and identity confusion. In this context, forming Christian young people committed to the Kingdom of God is not optional but an urgent command. As Proverbs 22:6 declares: "Train up a child in the way he should go, and even when he is old he will not depart from it." This biblical command drives us to sow eternal values into the next generations.

Holistic formation for young people must encompass three key dimensions: spiritual, intellectual, and moral. Only then can they respond with courage and discernment to the challenges of the contemporary world and become agents of cultural transformation.

The Challenges Facing Today's Youth

The current global culture has inherited a legacy of rapid change, influenced by technological advances and the dissolution of absolute truths. As Romans 1:25 warns, many have "exchanged the truth of God for a lie." This reality directly affects young people, who face challenges such as:

1. Identity Confusion: Cultural narratives seek to redefine what it means to be human, attacking the distinction between male and female and promoting a fluidity that contradicts God's design as described in Genesis 1:27: "God created mankind in his own image... male and female he created them."
2. Secularization of Knowledge: Educational institutions and mass media often portray faith as incompatible with science or reason, reinforcing the false divide between the spiritual and the rational.
3. Culture of Instant Gratification: Social media and technology have fostered a mindset of instant rewards, steering young people away from patience, effort, and the eternal purpose reflected in Hebrews 12:1-2.
4. Moral Relativism: In a world where truth is perceived as subjective, young people lack a clear moral compass to guide their daily decisions.

The Call to Active Discipleship

In response to these challenges, believers must rediscover and practice discipleship as a way of life. This process, as exemplified by Jesus, goes beyond teaching and involves modeling faith in everyday life. As Jesus said in Matthew 28:19-20: "Go and make disciples of all nations... teaching them to obey everything I have commanded you."

Key Strategies for Discipleship:

1. Deep Biblical Teaching: Help young people understand the fundamental principles of God's Word and how to apply them in their lives. This includes confronting cultural lies with the truth of Scripture (2 Timothy 3:16-17).
2. Community Practice: Create spaces where young people can experience the love of a Christian community that reflects the unity described in Acts 2:42-47.
3. Intergenerational Mentorship: Establish meaningful relationships between young people and adults who can impart wisdom and spiritual experience (Titus 2:6-8).

Christian Education as a Tool for Restoration

Education is not merely the transmission of knowledge but the holistic formation of character and spirit. Colossians 2:8 warns: "See to it that no one takes you captive through hollow and deceptive philosophy, which depends on human tradition." In this sense, Christian education must:

1. Integrate Faith and Knowledge: Recognize God as the source of all truth (Proverbs 2:6) and present the Bible as the foundation for learning in all areas of knowledge.
2. Foster Critical Thinking: Teach young people to analyze cultural narratives from a biblical perspective and defend their faith with sound arguments (1 Peter 3:15).
3. Promote Biblical Virtues: Instill values such as humility, justice, and service aligned with Christ's teachings (Micah 6:8).

Practical Proposals to Form a Transformative Generation

Equipping young people should not remain theoretical; it requires concrete and sustained actions:

1. Discipleship Groups: Establish programs where young people can share their struggles, learn biblical principles, and grow together in their walk with Christ.
2. Production of Christian Content: Create and promote digital media that present redemptive narratives and confront cultural relativism. Ephesians 4:29 exhorts: "Do not let any unwholesome talk come out of your mouths, but only what is helpful for building others up."

3. Community Service Initiatives: Encourage projects where young people can apply Christian values in their communities, showing Christ's love in action (Matthew 25:35-40).

The Promise of a Spirit-Filled Generation

The Bible is filled with examples of how God used young people to fulfill His purposes, from Samuel to Esther and Timothy. In Joel 2:28, God promises: "I will pour out my Spirit on all people; your sons and daughters will prophesy." This promise remains relevant, reminding us that young people can be agents of change if they are filled with the Holy Spirit.

Biblical Inspiration for Young People:

1. Joshua: He led Israel with courage and faithfulness, demonstrating that a life committed to God can impact an entire nation (Joshua 1:9).
2. Daniel: He stood firm in his faith in the midst of a pagan culture, showing that obedience to God brings favor and authority (Daniel 6:10-23).
3. Timothy: Though young, he was a key leader in the early church, exhorted by Paul not to let anyone despise his youth but to be an example to believers (1 Timothy 4:12).

A Generation That Will Transform Culture

The future of God's Kingdom on earth depends largely on how we prepare the coming generations. Equipping young people is not just a task; it is a mission from God. As the church, family, and community, we must take responsibility for discipling, educating, and launching a generation that not only survives cultural challenges but transforms them with the truth of the gospel.

Preparing the next generation is an eternal investment. May every young person we equip become a beacon of light in a dark world, a defender of truth in a time of confusion, and an ambassador of God's Kingdom, bringing hope and restoration wherever they go. As Philippians 2:15 declares: "So that you may become blameless and pure, children of God without fault in a warped and crooked generation. Then you will shine among them like stars in the sky."

A Call to Collective Action: The Church as an Agent of Transformation

"Make every effort to keep the unity of the Spirit through the bond of peace."
Ephesians 4:3

CHAPTER 16

A Call to Collective Action: The Church as an Agent of Transformation

The Unity of the Body of Christ in Action

The spiritual and moral restoration of society is a work that transcends individual efforts. As Christians, we are called to work together as a dynamic body, following the model of unity described in 1 Corinthians 12:12-27: "For just as the body is one and has many members, and all the members of the body, though many, are one body, so it is with Christ." This call to collective action is not only necessary but urgent in a culture that increasingly deviates from God's principles.

Christ made our collective mission clear in Matthew 28:18-20, the Great Commission: "Go and make disciples of all nations." This command is not limited to evangelism; it involves continuous discipleship that shapes cultures, systems, and hearts to reflect the Kingdom of God. It is a call to coordinated action, where each member of the body fulfills a unique but interdependent role with the common goal of glorifying God and expanding His Kingdom.

Discipleship: An Indispensable Strategy

Throughout this book, we have emphasized discipleship as a fundamental biblical tool. In previous chapters, we explored its application in the family, youth, and culture. Now, we must delve into its importance as a collective strategy for the church. Jesus gave us the perfect example by discipling a small group that, once equipped, transformed the world. In 2 Timothy 2:2, Paul instructs: "And the things you have heard me say in the presence of many witnesses entrust to reliable people who will also be qualified to teach others." This model of reproducible discipleship is key to cultural restoration.

The Role of the Local Church in Cultural Change

Local churches are the core from which cultural transformation must radiate. Each congregation has the potential to be a center for discipleship, equipping, and community action. To maximize this impact, churches must:

1. Promote Interdenominational Unity: Individualism and fragmentation among congregations are barriers that limit the reach of the Kingdom. Ephesians 4:3-6 exhorts us: "Make every effort to keep the unity of the Spirit through the bond of peace; there is one body and one Spirit, just as you were called to one hope."

Interdenominational collaboration allows churches to join forces to address complex social issues and present the Gospel comprehensively.

2. Equip Leaders and Members: Discipleship is not only for new believers; it is also essential to equip leaders and members with practical tools to influence their spheres of influence. This includes areas such as education, business, media, and politics. Colossians 1:28 says: "He is the one we proclaim, admonishing and teaching everyone with all wisdom, so that we may present everyone fully mature in Christ."

3. Develop Transformation Strategies: Churches must transition from being spaces of passive worship to centers of cultural action. This involves developing workshops, discipleship programs, community projects, and missionary efforts that reflect the values of God's Kingdom in practical and tangible contexts.

Shared Vision as a Catalyst for Change

A successful collective movement requires a clear and shared vision. Proverbs 29:18 reminds us: "Where there is no vision, the people perish." This vision must encompass all dimensions of life: family, work, education, politics, and culture. The church must intentionally articulate a vision that inspires believers to act in unity.

Examples of Collective Action

1. Church Networks: Establish local and global networks that coordinate efforts to address specific needs, such as educational programs, youth outreach, and advocacy for life and family.
2. Participation in Public Policy: Promote laws and policies aligned with biblical principles through Christian think tanks and action groups.
3. Community Discipleship: Form communities within churches that foster spiritual growth and equip believers to impact their contexts.
4. Production of Christian Media: Create audiovisual and digital content that confronts cultural lies with the truth of the Gospel.

Visionary Leadership for a Mobilized Church

The success of any movement depends on committed and Christ-centered leadership. Christian leaders must be examples of integrity, sacrifice, and service, following Jesus' model in Matthew 20:26-28: "Whoever wants to become great among you must be your servant." Visionary leadership inspires others to join the cause, mobilizing the church toward strategic and effective action.

Commitment to Truth

In a culture that celebrates relativism, commitment to truth must be unwavering. John 8:32 declares: "Then you will know the truth, and the truth will set you free." This commitment involves proclaiming truth in all public spheres and modeling a lifestyle that contrasts with current cultural trends. The church, as the bearer of divine truth, has the responsibility to be a beacon guiding society toward the light of Christ.

A Mobilized Church for the Glory of God

When the church works in unity, with vision and purpose, its impact is undeniable. This is the call of the Gospel: not only to save souls but to transform nations. Isaiah 60:1-3 exhorts us: "Arise, shine, for your light has come, and the glory of the Lord rises upon you."

As the body of Christ, we must embrace our responsibility to act collectively, knowing that every action, no matter how small, contributes to the fulfillment of God's plan for the redemption and restoration of His creation. The mobilized church, working as one body, can reflect God's justice, grace, and truth in all areas of society, thus fulfilling its eternal calling.

Back to
God's Design:
A Final Call to Restoration

"He will turn the hearts of the parents to their children, and the hearts of the children to their parents."
Malachi 4:6

CHAPTER 17

Back to God's Design: A Final Call to Restoration

The conclusion of this book is not merely the end of a reading journey but an urgent call to all believers to return to the perfect and eternal design God established for us. Throughout each chapter, we have explored how cultural trends, cinema, television, and modern ideologies have distorted the essential values God designed from the beginning. However, we have also discovered that this cultural challenge is not the final destination. At the heart of this cultural battle lies a deeper spiritual struggle—one that demands action, prayer, and a renewed commitment to the principles of God's Kingdom.

God's Design: Restoration, Unity, and Purpose

From creation, God instituted the family as the essential foundation of society and as a tangible reflection of His relationship with us. Genesis 2:24 declares: "For this reason, a man will leave his father and mother and be united to his wife, and they will become one flesh." This design not only unites man and woman in marriage but also creates an environment conducive to raising generations that model God's character.

The family is not an optional institution; it is the foundation of society and the primary instrument for passing on faith. Deuteronomy 6:6-9 affirms: "These commandments that I give you today are to be on your hearts. Impress them on your children." Yet, this design has been challenged by sin, secular ideologies, and systems of thought that seek to displace God from the center of our lives. Returning to God's design means restoring our families, our churches, and our societies under His lordship.

In Malachi 4:5-6, we find a powerful message of restoration: "He will turn the hearts of the parents to their children, and the hearts of the children to their parents." Just as Elijah was sent in times of apostasy, we are called to assume that same role in our generation—restoring relationships and bringing God's order to our families and communities.

An Eternal Vision: Living with Purpose and Expectation

As we fulfill our mission on earth, we must not forget that we are citizens of heaven. Philippians 3:20 declares: "But our citizenship is in heaven. And we eagerly await a Savior from there, the Lord Jesus Christ." The Christian life is not limited to the present; every action, word, and decision has eternal implications. We live with the hope of Christ's return, a promise that drives us to live with purpose and urgency.

Jesus warned us in Matthew 24:44: "So you also must be ready, because the Son of Man will come at an hour when you do not expect him." We are called to holiness, action, and spiritual preparation. Modern culture, saturated with evil and relativism, is a constant reminder that Christ's return is near. Therefore, our mission cannot wait; we must mobilize now to be an active, holy, and committed church.

A United Body to Transform the World

The work of restoration cannot be achieved in isolation. The Church, as the body of Christ, is called to be a beacon of light that illuminates darkness and transforms cultural structures with God's values. Ephesians 4:4-6 reminds us: "There is one body and one Spirit... one Lord, one faith, one baptism; one God and Father of all." This spirit of unity must be our strength to fulfill the collective mission of manifesting God's Kingdom on earth.

The unity of the Church is key to this restoration. As we have seen throughout this book, discipleship is the fundamental means to equip present and future generations. Whether through our families, our churches, or our spheres of influence, discipleship creates the foundation on which a strong church and a transformed society are built.

Key Areas of Collective Restoration

The Family as the Kingdom's Foundation: Restoration begins at home. It is the space where love, faith, and truth are modeled. Joshua 24:15 urges us: "As for me and my household, we will serve the Lord."

1. The Church as a Discipleship Center: Equip every believer to be an agent of change in their environment. Matthew 28:19 calls us: "Go and make disciples."

2. Culture as a Field of Influence: Use media, education, and politics to proclaim the truth. Romans 10:14 asks: "How can they hear without someone preaching to them?"

3. Service as a Reflection of Christ: Follow the example of Jesus, who did not come to be served but to serve (Matthew 20:28).

The Final Call: Salt and Light for a Needy World

Jesus called us to be salt and light in the world (Matthew 5:13-16). Being salt means preserving the values of truth, justice, and mercy in a decaying society. Being light means shining with the truth of Christ, dispelling the darkness of cultural lies and destructive ideologies. This call is not optional; it is a responsibility we must embrace with courage.

Steps to Action

1. Restore Our Homes: Establish times of prayer, fellowship, and Bible study as a family, modeling God's design in every aspect of our lives.
2. Mobilize Our Churches: Unite forces with other congregations to disciple, equip, and send leaders who will impact every sphere of society.
3. Use Media with Purpose: Leverage digital platforms, film, and television to proclaim truth and counter cultural lies.
4. Prepare for Christ's Return: Live with an eternal perspective, remembering that our actions here have eternal impact.

The Legacy of a Restored Generation

This book is not merely a reflection on the cultural challenges we face but a call to action. Every generation has the responsibility to be faithful to God's design, to disciple the next generation, and to prepare the way for the Lord's coming. Malachi 4:6 gives us a promise of reconciliation and restoration: "He will turn the hearts of the parents to their children, and the hearts of the children to their parents."

May this call inspire leaders, pastors, parents, and young people to rise with courage, proclaim the truth, and restore God's design in every corner of our society. On the glorious day of His coming, may we present ourselves as faithful servants, knowing we have fulfilled our calling and worked for His glory.

"For from Him and through Him and for Him are all things. To Him be the glory forever! Amen" (Romans 11:36).

BIBLIOGRAPHY

Books and Articles

- Chomsky, Noam, and Edward S. Herman. Manufacturing Consent: The Political Economy of the Mass Media. Pantheon Books, 1988.
- Overton, Joseph. "The Overton Window of Political Possibilities." Mackinac Center for Public Policy, 1996.
- Gramsci, Antonio. Selections from the Prison Notebooks. International Publishers, 1971.
- Lewis, C.S. The Abolition of Man. HarperOne, 1943.
- Schaeffer, Francis A. How Should We Then Live? The Rise and Decline of Western Thought and Culture. Crossway Books, 1976.
- Postman, Neil. Amusing Ourselves to Death: Public Discourse in the Age of Show Business. Penguin Books, 1985.
- Keller, Timothy. The Reason for God: Belief in an Age of Skepticism. Penguin Books, 2008.
- Guinness, Os. The Call: Finding and Fulfilling the Central Purpose of Your Life. Word Publishing, 1998.

Film and Media Studies

- Bordwell, David, and Kristin Thompson. Film Art: An Introduction. McGraw-Hill Education, 2016.
- Gerbner, George. "The Mainstreaming of America: Violence Profile No. 11." Journal of Communication, 1983.
- Jenkins, Henry. Convergence Culture: Where Old and New Media Collide. NYU Press, 2006.

Theological and Biblical References

- Carson, D.A. The God Who Is There: Finding Your Place in God's Story. Baker Books, 2010.
- Piper, John. Desiring God: Meditations of a Christian Hedonist. Multnomah Publishers, 2003.
- Wright, N.T. Simply Christian: Why Christianity Makes Sense. HarperOne, 2006.

Online Resources

- Mackinac Center for Public Policy. "The Overton Window." www.mackinac.org.
- Barna Group. Research Reports on Faith and Culture. www.barna.com.
- Pew Research Center. "Religion and Public Life." www.pewforum.org.
- Scriptural References

Additional Resources

- Kuby, Gabriele. La Revolución Sexual Global: La Destrucción de la Libertad en Nombre de la Libertad. Editorial Stella Maris, 2015.
- Díaz Araujo, Enrique. La Rebelión de la Nada. Material Exclusivo del Curso, 2017.

www.ingramcontent.com/pod-product-compliance
Lightning Source LLC
Chambersburg PA
CBHW061651250726
48659CB00004B/1460